I Talk to God About You.

40 Days of Prayer for My Future Husband

Written by Juanita I. Harris

Dedications

God

Willie and Virginia R. Harris

Mr. & Mrs. Layton E. Scoggins Sr.

Genita L. Harris

Rod Harris

Ruthie Harris

Willie Harris Jr.

Adrienne M. Brown

Pamela R. Hughey

Brandon L. Wilkins

My future husband.

Our children.

You.

Table of Contents

Table of Contents Cont'd

Foreword

The greatest thing one can do for God, self, and others is pray. I have an overwhelming amount of love, respect, and admiration for Juanita Harris. It has been a blessing over the course of many years to know Juanita, watch her grow, and see her mature as she has walked with the Lord and experienced God's redemptive and regenerating power through her prayer life. She has a remarkable and amazing ability to connect with others through her words, testimony, and writings, and in doing so, she reminds us that we are not alone.

In *I Talk to God About You,* Juanita speaks right to the heart of issues that daughters of the King experience when it comes to prayer, and she emphasizes how talking to our Father is the powerful key to unlocking intimacy with God. These personal prayers that are so lovingly shared, along with God's Word, will help guide and encourage you to persevere in prayer, even the prayers for your future husband and family.

So, no matter where you are on your spiritual journey, allow God to use this wonderful book of prayer and Scripture to help your prayer life come alive as you seek to know God more intentionally. Ask Him to do the miraculous. Prayer changes you. Prayer changes others. Let Juanita Harris show you how prayer changed her and her perspective on things yet to come! It blessed me, and I am confident it will bless you, too!

Mrs. Amy L. Covington
Director, Regener8 Ministries

Preface

"The Lord bless thee, and keep thee: The Lord make his face shine upon thee, and be gracious unto thee: The Lord lift up his countenance upon thee, and give thee peace."

Numbers 6:24-26, KJV

The scripture above is my sincere prayer for you. I was sitting in the reception area of my therapist's office when those words came to me. I had prayers but didn't have an introduction. When searching my heart for what to say, the Lord quietly spoke those words to me. There were many things that happened privately that caused me to seek out professional help.

One of them was the weight of my wait. There were many days that I felt like a public success and a private failure. Although I've won state teaching awards, am CEO of a growing benefit corporation, and a volunteer in my church and community, I struggle with dating relationships.

I never addressed the traumatic experiences in my life, so without my permission, each of my relationships did.

I am determined to be whole and take my best self into my marriage and into the lives of my children. My earnest prayer is to give them a childhood they do not have to recover from.

I have to give you this disclaimer, reading/praying these prayers cannot make God give you a husband or children. I wanted to make sure we talked about that before getting into the book. However, what I can guarantee is that in reading these, you will have an opportunity to share some quality time with God. In doing so, His word will wash over your heart. We could all benefit from that.

The more I searched the Word of God and prayed, the more I realized it was deeper than just connecting with someone. I need someone who will compliment the ministry of my life and vice versa. It is my prayer that you search the Word of God for yourself and pray the promises you find over your life.

Sharing these prayers is very therapeutic for me, and I thank you for being a part of my process.

Many of the prayers were written then revisited months later. The length of our prayers isn't near as important as the content. I pray you are inspired to pray. Whether you purchased this book for a friend or for yourself, know this, I am happy you're here and excited to pray with you.

Before you begin reading, please scan the QR code below to connect with our online community. We would love to walk alongside you for the next 40 days.

Prayer for my Sister in Christ

Dear Heavenly Father,

I pray for my sister in Christ as she grows through this 40-day devotional praying for my Brother in Love as well as herself. Lord, Your Word says if we confess our sins, You are faithful and just to forgive us our sins and to cleanse us from all unrighteousness. Help her to forgive herself too. Lord, if she has any unforgiveness in her heart, help her to release them and let it go.

If she is living contrary to Your Word, quicken her spirit in Jesus' name. Give her Godly wisdom that comes from You and You alone. Help her to honor You with every fiber of her being. When she speaks, touch her mouth and put Your words there just as You did for Jeremiah. I am asking that at this very moment, You consecrate her speech for Your use.

Lord allow her to see the importance of quality time with You. Let her make You a priority. If by chance my brother is reading this to see how we are praying for him, I pray all of these things over his life as well. It is in the mighty name of Jesus Christ, Son of the Most High God, that we submit this and every prayer.

SECTION 1

I Dedicate Him Back to YOU

Dear Heavenly Father,

Psalm 63:1-5 says O God, You are my God; early will I seek You; my soul thirsts for You, my flesh faints for You, in a dry and thirsty land with no water. I have seen You in the sanctuary, to see Your power and Your glory. Because Your loving kindness is better than life, my lips will praise You. Because of that, I bless You while I live; I will lift up my hands in Your name. My soul will be satisfied as with marrow and fatness, and my mouth will praise You with joyful lips.

There is something significant about seeking You early, which is why this prayer is being prayed at 5:52 am. God, You are everything to me and my soul longs to do and be what pleases You. Lord, last night in prayer, I made the decision to dedicate my future husband back to You. Lord, I know he is Yours and You'll only be loaning him to me for an allotted amount of time. Help me to honor him as I honor You! Help me to live a life publicly and privately that You are proud of. Let us worship You in spirit and in truth. Let the fragrance of our home be love, joy, peace, patience, kindness, goodness, and faithfulness too.

In Jesus Name

What will the fragrance of your home be?
How will you attain it?

Guard His Mind, Body, and Soul

Dear Heavenly Father,

I am praying for the mind of my husband. I am asking that You would dispatch angels to guard and guide him. Keep him from seducing spirits. Please allow him to seek You for all things. Comfort and consolation too. Don't let him find peace or comfort in drugs, alcohol, premarital sex, or any ungodly activities that are set up to draw his attention and heart away from You. Your word teaches us not to let anyone despise our youth. We are to be an example of the believers, in word, in conversation, in charity, in spirit, in faith, and in purity too.

Keep Your hand ever upon him. I come against every demonic attack that seeks to derail his destiny. I curse it at the root in Jesus' name and I plead the blood of Jesus over his life. I pray that today is one of the best days of his life. I pray that You would also bless his family too! I pray that if depression, anxiety, doubt, or fear try to take up residence that You would stop them at the door. In 2 Timothy 1:7, Your Word says that You didn't give us a spirit of fear, but of power, love, and a sound mind. Lord please bless him to fully embrace and walk in all three.

In Jesus Name

What's on your mind more than anything else? Can God be glorified through it?

Build Him Up

Dear Heavenly Father,

Thank You for my life and for my husband's as well. Mighty are the works of Your hands. I'm honestly in awe of You. Lord please do not allow my husband to struggle with depression or unworthiness. Build him up and equip him to fully walk in-and-out the purpose You've created him to achieve. Don't let him shrink; let him shine. If he should gain any acclaim, let him point people to Calvary. Let him be a Godly covering for our family!

Empower him to be the father he might not have ever seen. Allow me to love him unconditionally and forgive him automatically. Help me to honor him always. Lord, help my husband to love me in spite of me. Lord help me to let him love me. Lord, allow him to take the time to learn about me and help me to be an honest and open teacher. Sharing every piece of me...even the pieces that interfered with my peace. Help me to be emotionally naked before him and allow him to do the same before me. Help both of us to be mature and responsible with the information we receive.

In Jesus Name

Do you struggle with depression or unworthiness?
Why?

Cover Me as I Cover Him

Dear Heavenly Father,

Create in me a clean heart O God, and renew a right/steadfast spirit within me. Cast me not away from thy presence; and take not thy holy spirit from me. Lord, Your word teaches us not to live lives full of anxiety, but instead, we are to bring our requests to You in prayer with thanksgiving. Lord, thank You for the privilege of prayer. Thank You for always loving me, many times in spite of me. Thank You for keeping me the way that You do. Hebrews 13:4a teaches us that marriage is honorable in all and the bed undefiled.

Lord, my sincere prayer is to live a life that brings You honor and glory. You, O Lord, gave me the desire to be a wife and a mother. I ask that You continue to let the beauty of the Lord my God be upon me and bless the work of my hands. Keep me from growing weary in doing well. I will continue to take joy in You. I will continue to seek You first, knowing that all of these things (and many more) will be added to my life. I know that when the time is right, You will make it happen. I trust You.

In Jesus Name

Do you trust God enough to make it happen when the time is right? Why/Why not?

Lord, Do It.

Dear Heavenly Father,

I find comfort and direction in Your Word. Psalm 127:1 says, "Except the Lord build the house, they labour in vain that build it; except the Lord keep the city, the watchmen waketh in vain." Lord, I've made so many mistakes over the course of my lifetime. Thank You for continued sufficient grace and for renewing Your faithfulness toward me on a daily basis. Lord, if You do not build our marriage, it won't be built. If You don't keep us together, we won't be kept. All of the cute posts and likes will be in vain. Psalm 127:3 says, "Lo, children are an heritage of the Lord; and the fruit of the womb is his reward." Lord, please give us a heritage through my womb.

Lord, I am asking that You build my husband up in every area of his life. Where he lacks confidence, make him strong and courageous. Where he is confused, help him to trust You and remind him that Your Word is a lamp unto his feet and a light unto his path. Lord, the very same things I pray for and over the life of my husband, I pray for myself. Please continue to build my faith in You and help me continue to trust You with my whole heart.

In Jesus Name

What do you need the Lord to do?

SECTION 2

Lord, Heal the Trauma Too

Dear Heavenly Father,

Your word commands us to love one another as You have loved us. Lord, please equip my husband and I to die to ourselves so that powerful love is our reality. Help us to love You more than we love each other. In Isaiah 53:5, Your Word says, "but He was wounded for our transgressions, He was bruised for our iniquities: the chastisement of our peace was upon Him; and with His stripes we are healed."

Lord, help my husband heal from any trauma that interferes with him loving me purely and powerfully. Please help me do the same. The first step in any process is acknowledgment. Lord, help him recognize and identify the areas of his life that are damaged. Give him the strength to do the necessary work to become the best version of himself. Lord heal him and heal me too. I don't want us hurting each other because we've been hurt. Right now in the name of Jesus, I am asking that You break every dangerous and destructive cycle that has attempted to interrupt our lives year after year. It stops now!

In Jesus Name

What pain are you rehearsing that
needs God's healing?

Communication

Dear Heavenly Father,

Thank you for giving me the mind to pray. Your Word says the effectual fervent prayers of the righteous avail much. Help me to effectively communicate my heart to You. Help us to effectively communicate with each other. I thank You in advance for maturing me in that area. If he needs support in that area, please mature him as well. I pray that my husband's words would always land softly on the tablet of my heart.

I pray that when misunderstanding and offense try to take root, You would usher in a spirit of understanding and help me to find the truth in what my husband is expressing. Help us not to walk in or deliberately choose the spirits of offense or anger. I pray that he will always speak with wisdom and in truth. I pray that he is a leader among his peers. Proverbs 17:22a says, "A merry heart doeth good like medicine." With that truth in mind, I ask that he has a great sense of humor. I love you and most of all, I trust you.

In Jesus Name

What do you need to tell God?

Cleanse All Things

Dear Heavenly Father,

In every single thing, help me to give thanks: for this is the will of God in Christ Jesus concerning me. Please bless my husband with a grateful heart as well. Looking for You in every situation will keep Romans 8:28 at the forefront of our minds. We need to remember in good times, as well as those we deem bad, that all things work together for our good because we love You and are the called according to Your purpose. If this is an area he struggles in, help me to be a blessing to him in that area of his life.

Lord as I write to You, my prayer is that You would cleanse my husband's soul. Lord, let us both cleanse ourselves from all filthiness of the flesh and spirit, perfecting holiness in the fear of God. If we have any ungodly connections to women or men from our past, I curse them at the root and close all demonic portals open in our lives in Jesus' name. Please heal him from all trauma. If he needs to see a therapist, as I presently am, please connect him with one that is a perfect fit for him. Lord, destroy anything that would interfere with our relationship.

In Jesus Name

What is the most difficult situation you're facing right now? What is God teaching you through this moment?

A New Experience

Dear Heavenly Father,

Your Word says if any man be in Christ, he is a new creature: old things are passed away; behold, all things are become new. In the name of Jesus, I'm asking that my husband has a new beginning with You. I pray that leads him to his rightful place in You, and that place leads him to me.

Lord help me to be a good steward of his heart. Help me to honor him and You in all that I do. When I honor You, he will be honored as well. Help me to love him so well and so intentionally that his heart is safe with me, and he never has to question whether or not my motives are for the betterment of our family. Like the incredible woman described in Proverbs 31, let the heart of my husband trust safely in me as I lean and fully depend on YOU! Help me to do good and not evil to him all the days of my life. Help me to be a blessing to him and teach me how he needs to be loved.

In Jesus Name

Pray for the Salvation of your husband.

In Jesus Name

Search Our Hearts

Dear Heavenly Father,

Search me, O God, and know my heart: try me, and know my thoughts: And see if there be any wicked way in me, and lead me in the way everlasting. In the name of Jesus, I ask that You take charge of my husband's relationships and friendships. Place the right people in his path so that he grows, develops, and matures into the man of God that he needs to be to fulfill Your purpose and plan for our lives.

Lord, help me as a wife to submit myself to my husband, as unto You. We know the living picture of this is Christ. He is the head of the church and saviour of the body. Help us follow Your perfect example. When he falls short, as all have done, please help me to extend mercy to him and allow me to restore him in the spirit of meekness; considering myself in his shoes. Help me to do this, remembering that if it wasn't for the grace of God, I'd be in the same place. When I am in need of this mercy, please allow him to extend it to me in the same spirit of love and meekness.

In Jesus Name

Take a moment to search your heart
and your friendships.
What did you find?

SECTION 3

Prioritize Our Family

Dear Heavenly Father,

The first five words of 2 Kings 6:20 are "And it came to pass." Lord, I am asking for that same word to be spoken over our marriage. Lord, Please equip my husband to make our marriage a priority in a respectful way. I pray that his family embraces me and mine embraces him.

Although I pray our families get along, I pray we are able to successfully leave and cleave, understanding the importance of us leaving our families and cleaving to one another. Provide my husband with Godly examples. Fix it for me if it's not already as it should be. When decisions need to be made for the betterment of our home, please allow us to consult You and then each other first. Help us to trust YOU supremely and confidently. Help us to trust Your presence in each other. Help us to make decisions that will please You. Help us to share moment after moment of emotional intimacy. Please allow those moments to strengthen our relationship and draw us closer to You.

In Jesus Name

What are you believing God for? In other words, what are you expecting Him to do?

Mentor Him

Dear Heavenly Father,

Lord, I'm asking that You minister to my husband wherever he is. If he has been blessed with good Godly examples, I pray he would glean from them. If not, I have prayed that You would bless him with people after Your heart. David said, When my mother and father forsake me, the Lord will take me up. His parents hadn't forsaken him, but He was confident that even if that happened, You would care for him.

Lord, I do not know the details of my husband's relationship with his parents, but I have the same confidence in You that David did. If they forsook him, I know You took and will take him up. Thank you for this gift of singleness that we presently have. Although I think I am r-e-a-d-y to be married, bless us to use this time to focus on the things that bring You joy. Help us to devote time to becoming the absolute best version of ourselves during this season. Although the things that have happened to us are not our fault, allow us to be active participants in our healing, as that is our responsibility.

In Jesus Name

What is your relationship like with your parents? Are there any areas that need healing?

Develop His Taste Pallet

Dear Heavenly Father,

I just want to say thank You for loving me enough to create this man, my man, my husband, for me. Because of the trauma I experienced, I need a man who will speak softly to me, yet be man enough to take care of our home and children. Lord, I know that faith is the substance of things hoped for and the evidence of things not seen. Faith comes by hearing and hearing by the Word of God. It is my sincere prayer that my husband will hunger and thirst for righteousness. Even before we meet Father, I ask that He would hide Your words in his heart that he might not sin against You.

Please be his guiding compass. Thank You for giving me a husband who speaks words that are seasoned with kindness and motivated by love. You know all that my heart has been through. If he loves You and me, I will do everything in my power to be a repeated blessing to him, so much so it seems like it is never ending. In doing this, never let me lose sight of You, the Giver of every good and perfect gift. Thank You for answering my prayer.

In Jesus Name

Are you hungry and thirsty for righteousness?
What fruit in your life backs that up?

Walk in Love

Dear Heavenly Father,

I love and adore You! Please watch over my husband and I today. Fill our hearts with love, purpose, and peace. Help us to feel worthy of the love we deserve and bless us to be able to share that same love with the people around us. We love and trust You. Lord, I know me! You know him! Help us to be patient and kind to one another and not envious of each other. Help us not to think more of ourselves than what we should.

Lord, please don't allow us to get angry with one another quickly or demand our own way. Please do not let us rejoice in evil, but let us rejoice in truth. Father, don't allow us to be prideful or conceited but instead grace us to be caring and strong. Help us to bear all things, hope all things, and believe all things. We know that love never fails. Depending on what my husband has seen, he may have a hard time walking this out, and honestly, I may as well. Please comfort and correct us as we grow.

In Jesus Name

Read 1 Corinthians 13:4-9. How can you do a better job of walking in love?

Character Development

Dear Heavenly Father,

Thank You for being God. Thank You for loving me and being Lord over all aspects of my life. Including the details of my husband's character. Lord, You know exactly what we need to glorify You better together and I appreciate You for working out and on those things before we join as one. Lord be his 411 and 911. Mine too! Help him to seek You in all things now, so when we do come together and tough times come, his automatic turn is to You. Continue to work on his heart and mind, Father God. Your Word says we are supposed to be anxious for nothing, but in everything by prayer and supplication, with thanksgiving, let our requests be made known to You.

Lord, if he is an anxious person, as I have been, I ask that You minister to him at this moment. Help him to trust You fully and pray to You often. Help him to know that You can and beyond that, help him to know that You will. Lord, You know just how anxious I've been about meeting, loving, and being loved by him. I ask that You'd help me to find joy in the journey as I wait for the manifestation of my prayers. Help us to never lose sight of You being our epicenter.

In Jesus Name

What are you anxious about? Have you prayed about it yet? Give it to God on the lines below. Leave it there too.

In Jesus Name

SECTION 4

Seed to the Sower

Dear Heavenly Father,

Although we didn't grow up with a lot of money, my Mother was a good steward of what we had. Those invaluable lessons are still shaping me today. Please bless my husband to be a good steward of our money. If he has a paycheck to paycheck mentality, I pray that it be broken in the mighty and matchless name of Jesus Christ. There will be no lack in our home. We will always have an abundance and will give from our overflow. We will have delicious home-cooked meals on a regular basis and enjoy each other's company.

I pray that You bless the work of our hands and give us multiple streams of income. Lord, help him to be wise with investing. Help him to be like the servant in the parable found in Matthew 25:16-17. Let the spirit of multiplication be heavy on his life. Give him Godly wisdom and favor. I am asking that he be anointed for expansion.

In Jesus Name

What part of your mentality needs a makeover?

Living Epistles

Dear Heavenly Father,

I pray that You speak to and massage the very heart of my husband. If we have to fight, let it be against satan in pursuit of Your truth. Lord, I honor You. I praise You and ask that You would remove selfish pride from both of our hearts. Do not let us do anything through strife or for vainglory; but in lowliness of mind, let us regard each other better than ourselves.

If there is anything that is hindering our growth and development, I curse it at the root and bind it in the name of Jesus. We need YOU. We need You like fish need water to breathe. We need You like birds need the sky to travel through. We need You like a sail needs wind to work at its optimum. WE NEED YOU. Let us never lose sight of that truth.

In Jesus Name

Take a moment to reflect quietly. Is there anything that is hindering your growth as a Christian and a wife-to-be?

Break the Addictions

Dear Heavenly Father,

Please guard my husband's mental, physical, spiritual, and emotional health. I am concerned because so many men are taught not to cry and aren't allowed to feel. Lord if he is battling any addictions, I ask that you break them in Jesus name. Allow him to think about You, Your desires, and Your will above all.

Strengthen him and monitor his public and private activity. If he is struggling with an addiction to pornography, please surround him with Christian men to help him through it.

In Jesus Name

What is your mental, physical, spiritual, and emotional health like? Are you struggling with any addictions?
Let's take it to God in prayer.

In Jesus Name

Salvation and Integrity

Dear Heavenly Father,

Your Word teaches us if we confess with our mouth that Jesus is Lord and believe in our heart that You, God, have raised Him from the dead, we shall be saved. Lord, I do not know the status of my husband's relationship with You, nor do I know whether or not he has given both his life and heart to You. Lord, at this moment, I pray salvation and surrender over his life. I pray that if he has given his life to You but has compromised his walk along the way, as all of us have, that he would rededicate his life soon!

I pray that if he is accustomed to making things happen/going at life on his own, that he would fully surrender his heart and will to You. Yielding an invention to the creator is always the best idea. I do not mind submitting to him. I want him to be the head of our home and the leader in every possible way. I long for the day that I can lay my hands on him, and pray for him as he sleeps. I long for the day he does the same for me and our babies too. Thank You for allowing me to live to see this day. Please allow integrity to be synonymous with my husband's name. Please help him to keep his eyes on You and help him to seek to honor You in all that he does.

In Jesus Name

Are there any areas of your life that you need to surrender to Christ? What does your quiet time with Christ look like?

Present of YOUR Presence

Dear Heavenly Father,

My future husband needs Your presence in his life. Keep him holy Father God. Surround him with good solid friends who will encourage him in the ways of righteousness and not down the path of sin and shame. Please sever any present soul ties and keep him from making any new ones. Please keep Your hands on him. Help him to make decisions that will please You and that will honor me and our marriage. Massage his heart and open his mind even now.

In areas where he may have compromised and given in to the desires of his flesh, I ask that You give him an overwhelming sense of conviction. Don't let him make the same mistakes over and over again. I know that everyone has a different path, but I am asking that You'd straighten him out if need be. While You're tending to him, please remember me. I've not always made the right choices and I struggle more than anyone knows. Thank You for delivering me from the bondage of my past and keeping me until the appointed time.

In Jesus Name

What shape is your soul in? Does it need a detox?

SECTION 5

Embracing Love

Dear Heavenly Father,

Thank You for the many ways You command Your love toward us. Please let my husband fully embrace and know love because he knows You. Please let him constantly search for and implement new ways to show me that he loves me and please do not let him be afraid to touch me. Please let him enjoy writing love notes. Please let me learn how he desires to be loved and operate fully in that space.

Please let him have a hunger for how I need to be loved and walk therein. Give him the verbal passcodes for spaces I've not granted anyone access to. While You're helping and teaching him how to love me, please teach me how to do the very same for him. Help me to speak and demonstrate how he needs to be loved fluently so that he knows You sent me to him.

In Jesus Name

Are you prepared to love someone the way they need and not how you want to love them?

Generous Servant

Dear Heavenly Father,

Your Word says give and it shall be given unto you; good measure, pressed down, and shaken together, and running over, shall men give into your bosom. For with the same measurement that we measure, it shall be measured to you again. There have been times in my life when I wished I wasn't so generous because it felt like people were taking advantage of me. Now I have peace because I know You created me this way. You know my heart is huge when it comes to serving and giving to Your people.

Lord, please bless my husband to have a generous heart as well. I pray that he has a heart for serving and giving to others so that there won't be conflict surrounding opportunities to operate in that part of who I am. Please equip him with an enduring and patient spirit. Please develop him as a manager of all things in our home and our ministry. Lord, please bless him to be patient with me. I have experienced a lot of trauma, and even now as I write this prayer, I'm still growing through a lot. Allow him to seek You with diligence so he will know how to protect and properly handle me.

In Jesus Name

When was the last time you operated in generosity? How will this be seen in your home?

Jesus Centered

Dear Heavenly Father,

Please help us to always keep Jesus at the center of our marriage. It is possible that neither one of us had an in-house example of what that looks like. Because of that, we aren't starting from a template but from experiences. Some of which I'd like to forget. Lord, because of what I saw, I struggle heavily with trust and abandonment issues. I also dabble in self-sabotage, but You know that. There have been times when I've intentionally tried to mess up relationships in my past and You've intervened. Please do the same in my marriage. When I'm afraid, only You know what I'll do.

Please knit my heart with my husband's. Please allow me to be taken care of in my marriage so that I don't look outside of my husband and both negatively and selfishly involve others to meet the needs that he is supposed to. Please help us to always seek You first. Please give us Godly examples which can give us guidance. Please allow them to be open, honest, and transparent with us. Please let them share their wisdom generously and allow them to give us practical ways to apply the truths. Lord, it is my desire for You to be our everything.

In Jesus Name

In what areas of your life do you desperately need the Holy Spirit?

Godly Friendships

Dear Heavenly Father,

Before I ask You for anything, I would like to thank You for everything. Lord, please surround my husband with Godly friends. Please surround him with Godly honorable, trustworthy, and faithful men of God. Lord, please allow them to walk in the kind of integrity that would make my husband a better man.

Please let them be honest with him. Please let them walk in such a way that holiness is common and not far-fetched at all. I trust You to give me a husband that I won't have to recover from. Please watch over him as he rests and satisfy him with long life.

In Jesus Name

Do you have mentors and Godly
friendships that add value to your life?
Describe them below.

Psalm 91

Dear Heavenly Father,

Psalm 91 says He that dwelleth in the secret place of the most High shall abide under the shadow of the Almighty. Lord, please bless my husband to know that You're his refuge and his fortress: his God. Help him to trust in You. I'm confident that You'll deliver him from the snare of the fowler and from the noisome pestilence. You'll cover him with Your feathers, and under Your wings shall he trust. Your truth shall be his shield and buckler. He won't be afraid of the terror by night; nor for the arrow that flieth by day. Nor of the pestilence that walketh in darkness. Nor of the destruction that wasteth at noonday. A thousand shall fall at his side, and ten thousand at his right hand; but it shall not come near him. Only with his eyes will he behold and see the reward of the wicked because he has made You his refuge, even the Most High, his habitation. Lord, Your Word goes on to say that no evil befall him, neither shall any plague come nigh his dwelling. This is so because You'll give Your angels charge over him, to keep him in all his ways. The angels shall bear him up in their hands, lest he dash his foot against a stone. He shall tread upon the lion and adder: the young lion and the dragon shalt he trample under his feet. Because You have set Your love upon him, therefore, You'll deliver him: You'll set him on high, because he hath known Your name. He shall call upon You, and You'll answer him: You'll be with him in trouble; You'll deliver him, and honour him. With long life, You'll satisfy and show him Your salvation.

In Jesus Name

Read Psalm 91 in a few different translations and write down what you understand below.

SECTION 6

Sexual Purity

Dear Heavenly Father,

Sexual sin is one of those things that will take you farther than you want to go and keep you longer than you intend to stay. Lord, if my husband is struggling with masturbating, deliver him. If he is struggling with fornication, help him to flee. If he has an addiction to pornography, please minister to and deliver him from that vice grip of a stronghold in Jesus name. I plead the blood over his life, internet use, and daily interactions! I thank You for the deliverance that is taking place in his life even now. While You're ministering to him, please do not pass me by. You've been gracious enough to always place me in the care of men who respect my decision to abstain until marriage.

Lord, help me to respect me. Help me maintain my purity until You give me the last name of the man of Your dreams for me. I don't want to have the testimony that it just happened or that I couldn't help myself. I know that You will forgive me for my sins, but please do not allow me to take that grace for granted. Stand in my way. Dispatch angels. Cancel my plans. Whatever it takes to keep me pure, do it. I give You full consent to intervene. Society is inundated with constant images and suggestions of sexual perversion. Be his shield. Be my shield. Be our shield.

In Jesus Name

Are you secretly struggling with sexual sin?
Write out a prayer asking God for assistance
that only he can give!

In Jesus Name

Goals

Dear Heavenly Father,

Like the Proverbs 31 Woman, I am wired to work. I came up watching my mother work and it instilled a strong work ethic in my heart. I pray that my husband is goal-oriented and ambitious. I pray that people trust and desire to be around him. Please allow his love for You to shine through in every task that he takes on. Please give him the wisdom to know when to work and when to come home.

Please allow him to work just as hard in our home and he works on his job. Just like goals are set for our careers and finances, let us set goals for growth toward things that please You and that will bring us closer together. Allow us to work hand-in-hand, and bone-in joint for Your glory. Help us to grow into what we've possibly never seen. I know what I saw. I cannot speak about his experience, but what I can ask is that You'd mentor us. Teach us Your precepts. Help us Lord. It's possible both of us are starting from experiences that we don't want to recreate. Give us the desire to work in our homes just as hard as we work in the world.

In Jesus Name

Set 3 goals this week:
1 personal, 1 professional, and 1 for your devotional time with God (aside from this book).

Patient Teacher

Dear Heavenly Father,

Please massage my husband's heart and mind. Please prepare his heart to be patient with me and teach me in love. Please prepare my heart in love. Create patience in me that is exclusively for him. I want him to honor me with gentle instruction, so please prepare me to do and be the same. You know what I've been through that I do not discuss. You know the silent tears that I've cried. You know the destructive thoughts that began to plague me in my 20's and resurfaced again in my 30's. Because of all of the things that have been done to me, and all that I've done to myself, it's going to take YOU helping me so that I don't destroy what You give me. I'm an incredible friend. Help me to be a help meet and a blessing. Much of what I desire, I didn't grow up seeing. Many were negatively impacted by the pandemic, but me? I was negatively impacted by my past. I'm still recovering. Help me Lord. I want to be fruitful and multiply. I want to have a home where we serve You. I want to have a home where Your steadfast love never ceases and is new every morning. I've grieved You enough, but if You don't help me soon, I'm going to inadvertently add more things I have to repent for. Please send help.

In Jesus Name

What do you need God to do in your heart? If you don't know, ask the Holy Spirit to intercede.

Holiness

Dear Heavenly Father,

Please let my husband walk in the Holy Spirit. Please help me to do the same. Do not allow either one of us to perfect any behaviors as single people that will destroy our marriage. In our dating relationships, help us to be honest, vulnerable, trustworthy, and faithful. Hold our feet to the fire, and in doing so, hold us to a higher standard in You. Lord, I know the type of men that I am attracted to, just as there is a certain type of woman that my husband is attracted to.

Lord, don't let that proclivity of a bias go without boundaries. Help us to utilize wisdom even now! Give us a solid foundation through a friendship where You are nucleus, core, and epicenter all in one! Be our guard and our shield. Lord, please let all that we do be done in love. Please disarm our triggers tied to trauma, and let us lean on You as our source. Because of my past, I am prone to running away when challenges come, and maybe my husband is too. When the time is right, let us run right into each other! I know that You can and will make it happen. Let us take delight in You knowing that You will give us the desires of our hearts. Please don't let us be wise in our own eyes.

In Jesus Name

Are you developing any behaviors as a single person that have the potential to destroy your marriage?

Respect

Dear Heavenly Father,

Ephesians 5:33 teaches wives to respect their husbands. Lord, help me with this. Even in my singleness, build me up in this area. Monitor my behavior in public and private spaces. Do not let me get too close to any man that isn't my husband—no sleepovers or anything close to it. Ruin my plans if they even come close to spending late nights and early mornings with a man who hasn't given me his last name.

I am not used to being able to trust many people and I despise group projects from my innermost being! Sink or swim, pass or fail; I'd rather do it alone. By your grace and mercy, I'm used to making things happen that way. It's difficult and uncomfortable to depend on others. Lord, the last thing I want to do is disrespect and dishonor my husband. You know me; the me that no one else knows. Please keep me. Beyond that, help me not to dishonor You anymore than I already have. I know all have sinned and come short of your glory, but I don't want to use grace as an excuse to continue in sin. As I've prayed so many times, please help me.

In Jesus Name

Have you asked God to help you with you today? Take a moment to candidly share your struggles with him on the lines below.

SECTION 1

Weight of the Wait

Dear Heavenly Father,

I am encouraged by Psalm 27:13-14. Like David, I'm confident I too, would have fainted had I not believed to see the goodness of the Lord in the land of the living. The weight of the wait gets heavy sometimes, but I will continue to wait on You Lord and be of good courage while doing so. This will be my position because Your word says You shall strengthen my heart. Your Word tells us that if it is good, You won't withhold it from those who walk upright. If it's withheld, I know it's either not good for me, or I'm out of alignment. Either way, Your will is best and I trust You.

Lord, I want to experience all of the goodness that a life fully emerged in You has to offer. Help me to walk, talk, and live in a way that will please You. Lord Your Word also teaches us that when a man finds a wife he finds a good thing and obtains favor from the Lord. Please direct my husband to me so that He can obtain his favor from You. I am ready to help him birth the desires You've placed in his heart. Equip me even now to be a blessing and not a burden to him. Teach me how to love, empower, and inspire him. Help me to bring out the absolute best in him on a daily basis.

In Jesus Name

What do you need the Lord to teach you to do?

Anoint His Hands

Dear Heavenly Father,

Your Word says, "Likewise the Spirit also helpeth our infirmities: for we know not what we should pray for as we ought: but the Spirit itself maketh intercession for us with groanings which cannot be uttered. And he that searcheth the hearts knoweth what is the mind of the Spirit because he maketh intercession for the saints according to the will of God". I thank You for this and ask that You help me intercede for my husband. You know his beginning, his present, his future, and his end. Because You are God, I'm asking that we leave no stone unturned in prayer.

Cover him God, from the crown of his head to the very soles of his feet. Anoint his hands and put miracles in his mouth. Allow him to speak Your will and see things be established in Jesus Name. Help us to maximize every moment we have. Give us hearts of understanding. Lord, I'm asking that at this very moment, You'd download Your Word to our hearts. Having Your word close will help us through any challenge that arises. Lord, when we don't know what to pray, please speak directly to our hearts. We are here and attentively listening.

In Jesus Name

Write a prayer for your husband!

In Jesus Name

Blessings Tied to Tithing

Dear Heavenly Father,

I pray for the finances of my husband even now as a single person. Lord, if he has made some costly mistakes with his credit, I ask that You'd pair him with someone who is honest and trustworthy to help him clean things up. Please allow him to be teachable and receptive to the instructions he's given. When his credit is in good condition, please equip him with the necessary tools to maintain it. Keep legacy in his view and remind him that his finances aren't just important for his now, but our next too. Your Word teaches us in Malachi 3:10-11 to bring all of our tithes into the storehouse, that there may be meat in Your house. You went on to pronounce a blessing over us, letting us know that You would in turn, open the windows of Heaven and pour out a blessing that there would not be enough room for us to receive. You went on to say that You would rebuke the devourer for our sakes and that You would not destroy the fruits of our ground; neither shall our vine cast her fruit before the time in the field. Lord, help us to be recipients of those guarantees. Your record is sure. Your Word is absolute! I rest on it and in You. Keep your hand on us and our wallets too.

In Jesus Name

How can you become more financially sound?
Let's pray about it below.

In Jesus Name

Safely Trust

Dear Heavenly Father,

I need Your strength to be made perfect in my weakness. I do not know how my husband processes hurt and grief. My heart is heavy and I need you to comfort him wherever he is. My flesh wishes he was near so I could hold him in my arms when he goes through difficult times and pray for him both in my heart and out loud. Lord, I trust You to be the God that heals. I need You to wrap him in Your arms since I can't. I don't know if he has been taught not to cry, but just like the husband in Proverbs 31, help his heart to trust safely in me.

Make me an honorable wife that is responsible with his heart. If he isn't comfortable releasing, place a drawing anointing on my life, and by the power of the Holy Ghost, allow me to pull those things out of him that he tries to hide from others so that He can heal in Jesus name. I am sure that my husband allows the people around him to cry, and I ask that you give him that same grace to feel. Please establish our home to be a safe place for us. Allow our home to be a place we are comfortable falling apart because we know we will be lovingly restored.

In Jesus Name

How do you process hurt and grief?
Is this healthy for you and those connected to you? Let's pray.

In Jesus Name

The Enemy (Inner Me)

Dear Heavenly Father,

From everlasting to everlasting, thou art God. Lord, I come in humility and boldness. I come humbly because of who You are, yet boldly because I am confident in You. I am insecure. I can hide it from everyone but you. I've been praying diligently for my future husband; however today, I am in need. I don't know if I should blame the enemy or the inner me. One day, I'll be completely healed from the pain of my past, but my present reality is that I am afraid. Afraid that I won't measure up. Afraid that I will mess things up. Afraid that I will hurt the man that You bless me with.

Your word teaches us not to be afraid because You are with us. Help me to realize and internalize that truth so that I can walk in a boldness that only You can give. I want to be happy, healthy, and whole for real this time. Lord, I know that true happiness and contentment are found in You. Help me to walk and live in that space even after I get married. I do not want to depend on anyone for my happiness, and I need You to help me stabilize my emotions. Help me not to develop codependency on anyone for happiness. Help me to be right within.

In Jesus Name

What do you need to pray about
that you don't discuss?

In Jesus Name

SECTION 8

Hide & Seek

Dear Heavenly Father,

Proverbs 25:2 says, " It is the glory of God to conceal a thing: but the honour of kings is to search out a matter." Lord, as I study Your Word, I ask that You equip me with the knowledge hidden there. God it is my sincere desire to be all that You've called me to be. It is also my desire to see my husband become all that You've called him to be. God, I ask that You'd expose him to me, and me to him. Let there be no secrets between us. Give me the strength to study him and find him wherever he is literally or figuratively speaking. Allow my spiritual GPS to be heightened. Before danger even manifests in either of our lives. Drop it in my spirit, and allow my posture to be prayer. Please heighten my discernment and allow my relationship with You to continually bear fruit. Please do the same for my husband. Allow me to willfully submit to him. I will follow him as he follows You without hesitation or reservation. I humbly submit to You, oh God. Please strengthen our resolve so that we do not lose steam in the middle of the battle. Fill us with You oh Lord. Help us to never get tired of locating each other. Don't let us drift in any sense of the words. If we begin to walk by sight and not by faith, correct and redirect us.

In Jesus Name

Are you going to be committed to the covenant between you and your husband, or will you only stay as long as things are convenient?

Prayer Life

Dear Heavenly Father,

There are times, like now, when I come before you and I have no clue what to say. All I know for certain is that I'm supposed to be here, in your presence, at this moment. I'm sure my husband has experienced or is experiencing the very same. No matter how many times our words escape us, please always give us a mind to pray. Your Word teaches us how to fast in Matthew 6:17-18.

We're supposed to anoint our heads and wash our faces so that it doesn't appear to men that we are fasting, but unto You, Our Father which is in secret: and You, Our Father, see what we do in secret, and reward us openly. Help us fast and pray. Help us consult You first and foremost as individuals and as a couple. Help us to seek You about everyday decisions and those we deem big! We want to be close to You and always in your will. Always.

In Jesus Name

When was the last time you fasted and prayed?
In what ways did God meet you there?

Ephesians 5

Dear Heavenly Father,

In Ephesians 5, Your Word teaches us that the husband is the head of the wife, even as Christ is the head of the church: and He is the saviour of the body. As the church is subject to Christ, we are to be the same to our own husbands in everything.

Lord, please let my husband fully surrender to You. I have no problem submitting to a man who is submitted to You. I enjoy making waves on my own but being strong all the time is exhausting. As much as I despise group work, it would be nice to have someone I could truly depend on. Help us to love ourselves and each other from the purest places that we have. Help us to love You above all. Love covers a multitude of sins. Please give us a heavy and never ending blanket of love.

In Jesus Name

Have you fully surrendered every area
of your life to God?

Heaven on Earth

Dear Heavenly Father,

When I was young, I learned to pray. "Our Father which art in heaven, Hallowed be thy name. Thy kingdom come, Thy will be done in earth, as it is in heaven. Give us this day our daily bread. And forgive us our debts, as we forgive our debtors. And lead us not into temptation, but deliver us from evil: For thine is the kingdom and the power, and the glory, forever." Lord, I know Heaven on Earth is possible because Your Word laid it out in this template. Lord, let your kingdom come.

Lord let Your will be done on earth as it is in Heaven. Let Your hand of provision and protection rest on our home. Please forgive us as we forgive and do not let us be led into temptation. The kingdom, power, and glory are all Yours forever! Lord, I don't know what Heaven on Earth feels like, but I'm asking that You grant me this desire as it is in my heart. Please allow my husband, children, and all that are connected to me to experience it.

In Jesus Name

Do you want to experience Heaven on Earth?
Talk to God about it on the lines below.

In Jesus Name

The Benediction

Dear Heavenly Father,

You are able to do exceeding abundantly above all that we ask or think, according to the power that worketh in us, unto You be glory in the church by Christ Jesus throughout all ages, world without end.

In Jesus Name
Amen

Do you believe that God is able to exceed your expectations? Do you trust that He will?

ENCOURAGEMENT

When we began this journey 40 days ago, I spoke the following blessing over your life.

"The Lord bless thee, and keep thee: The Lord make his face shine upon thee, and be gracious unto thee: The Lord lift up his countenance upon thee, and give thee peace."
Numbers 6:24-26 KJV

The scripture above was and still is my sincere prayer for you. I was sitting in the reception area of my therapist's office when those words came to me. Four days from this moment, I will be in the reception area of my therapist's office once more.

When searching my heart for what to say, the Lord quietly spoke those words to me. Now that we are at the end, he took me back to the beginning. Funny how that works.

As I mentioned before, there are many things that happened privately that caused me to seek out professional help, and much of it flowed from my heart as I pinned each of the prayers found on the pages of this book.

Know that you aren't alone on this journey. I love you and am praying for you.

Stay committed to becoming the absolute best version of yourself that you can. Your prayer life and mental health are priorities.

Please do not neglect either of them.

Be Blessed!
Juanita I. Harris

P.S. Keep reading.

How Do You See You?

When my publisher asked if I had 20 more pages in me, I was very hesitant and gave an excuse that almost worked. However, when God has a will, He will cover the bill. As mentioned on the previous pages, I had a session with my therapist this afternoon.

The question at the top of this page was posed in so many words, and my answer was, "broken." Moments later, she picked up a glass dish and said, "If I drop this can it be repaired?" My answer was, "No. It will be shattered." Then she picked up a plastic water bottle and said, "What happens when I drop this?" My response was, "It gets dented, but it can be popped back into place." She nodded.

It was at that moment that things began to come together for me. She gently explained that the things that happened to and around me weren't my fault, but healing by doing the hard work was necessary.

Then she said something that I never anticipated, "Congratulations." She affirmed me in that moment of breakthrough and my life will never be the same. She encouraged me to be mindful of how I speak of myself because it truly matters.

Before I left the session, my proclamation had changed from "I'm broken" to "I'm becoming." Scripture says it this way, "Therefore if any man be in Christ, he is a new creature: old things are passed away; behold, all things are **become** new."

Everyone has a past, but we have an opportunity at a new life in Christ. The last thing I want you to walk away from this book thinking is that I have it all together. I don't. I am a sinner who was in need of the saving grace that only comes through accepting Jesus Christ as my Lord and Savior. I am sure I shared this before, but we can definitely share it again.

Romans 10:9-10 says, "That if thou shalt confess with thy mouth the Lord Jesus, and shalt believe in thine heart that God hath raised him from the dead, thou shalt be saved. For with the heart, man believeth unto righteousness; and with the mouth, confession is made unto salvation." Our goal is to know Christ and make Him known.

So many of us, myself strongly included, have listened to what the world/social media has said about who we are. Please rest assured that everyone isn't as happy as they post to be. Read that sentence one more time.

The closer we get to Christ, the more we unearth about who we truly are, and thus we are inspired to become. Isn't that good news?

If you are reading this, I am encouraging you to do two things; get serious about your relationship with God and your relationship with yourself. If you need to seek out professional help, do it! We invest in everyone around us without a second thought. Make provisions for you, too.

Instead of believing the lies satan whispers, or what popular culture says is acceptable, spend some quality time in your Bible. My sincere prayer is that if you have ever referred to yourself as broken, you will shift your confession just as I have to becoming. If you have committed to doing the hard, necessary, and sometimes ugly work that is required, your future will be better and brighter because of what you've decided here today.

We will no longer exist but thrive. In Jesus Name Amen (It is so)

Congratulations!

Made in the USA
Las Vegas, NV
08 November 2023

80485940R00061